My Own Show

A Play

Lesley Bruce

A Samuel French Acting Edition

SAMUELFRENCH-LONDON.CO.UK
SAMUELFRENCH.COM

Copyright © 2007 by Lesley Bruce
All Rights Reserved

MY OWN SHOW is fully protected under the copyright laws of the British Commonwealth, including Canada, the United States of America, and all other countries of the Copyright Union. All rights, including professional and amateur stage productions, recitation, lecturing, public reading, motion picture, radio broadcasting, television and the rights of translation into foreign languages are strictly reserved.

ISBN 978-0-573-11263-8

www.samuelfrench-london.co.uk

www.samuelfrench.com

FOR AMATEUR PRODUCTION ENQUIRIES

UNITED KINGDOM AND WORLD
EXCLUDING NORTH AMERICA
plays@SamuelFrench-London.co.uk
020 7255 4302/01

Each title is subject to availability from Samuel French,

depending upon country of performance.

CAUTION: Professional and amateur producers are hereby warned that *MY OWN SHOW* is subject to a licensing fee. Publication of this play does not imply availability for performance. Both amateurs and professionals considering a production are strongly advised to apply to the appropriate agent before starting rehearsals, advertising, or booking a theatre. A licensing fee must be paid whether the title is presented for charity or gain and whether or not admission is charged.

The professional rights in this play are controlled by The Agency Ltd, 24 Pottery Lane, Holland Park, London W11 4LZ.

No one shall make any changes in this title for the purpose of production. No part of this book may be reproduced, stored in a retrieval system, or transmitted in any form, by any means, now known or yet to be invented, including mechanical, electronic, photocopying, recording, videotaping, or otherwise, without the prior written permission of the publisher. No one shall upload this title, or part of this title, to any social media websites.

The right of Lesley Bruce to be identified as author of this work has been asserted by her in accordance with Section 77 of the Copyright, Designs and Patents Act 1988

MY OWN SHOW

First presented at the Stephen Joseph Theatre, Scarborough, on 22nd August 2006 with the following cast:

Fay	Maggie Ollerenshaw
Jude	Gabrielle Lloyd
Gillian	Susan Twist
Bollards	Gillian Hanna
Allan	Ian Midlane

Directed by Deborah Bruce
Décor by Simon Rorstand
Lighting by Jo Dawson

CHARACTERS

Fay
Jude } 45-55, but the same age as each other
Gillian
Bollards
Allan, Bollards' son, sixteen years younger

The action of the play takes place in the living-room of Fay's house, which doubles as a chat show studio

SYNOPSIS OF SCENES

ACT I
S<small>CENE</small> 1   Fay's sitting-room
S<small>CENE</small> 2   The same. Moments later
S<small>CENE</small> 3   The same. A little later
S<small>CENE</small> 4   The same. Moments later
S<small>CENE</small> 5   The set of *Frankly Fay*

ACT II
S<small>CENE</small> 1   Fay's sitting-room. Several weeks later
S<small>CENE</small> 2   The same. Soon afterwards
S<small>CENE</small> 3   The same. That night
S<small>CENE</small> 4   The set of *Frankly Fay*
S<small>CENE</small> 5   Fay's living-room
S<small>CENE</small> 6   The same. Not very much later
S<small>CENE</small> 7   The set of *Candidly Caroline*
S<small>CENE</small> 8   Fay's living-room

Time — the present

ACT I

Scene 1

Fay's sitting-room

There are three exits, one to the kitchen, one to the front door and the rest of the house, and one to the stairs, the bottom few of which are visible. The room is decorated in clear colours and furnished with big modern sofas and chairs, a glass coffee table, a drinks cupboard and a television. There is a cordless phone. It is like a chat-show set

When the play begins, a big red leatherbound book lies on the table. Fay, Gillian and Jude are on stage; they have just come in. Fay lies in a foetal position on a sofa. Gillian and Jude stand around helplessly, looking down at her. They are all still in their coats

Gillian We thought you'd be pleased. We thought you'd love it. They wrote and asked us. And we said carry on, go ahead, she's bound to be delighted.
Jude I would. I'd be over the moon. I'd be completely ecstatic.
Fay (*raising her head briefly*) What makes you think they'd do you?
Jude They wouldn't. Of course they wouldn't. I just meant if they did.
Fay You're a total nonentity, no-one's ever heard of you, why would they want to do you?
Gillian You've been moaning on for years about being overlooked. And now you're not. You're not overlooked. (*She grabs up the red book; whispering*) This week you find me backstage at the Duchess Theatre, waiting to meet a lady who has been fighting our corners, exposing our issues and righting our wrongs for almost twenty years. She may not always be a comfortable voice but she is always a respected one and there are few in her profession — ah, here she comes, if I can just manage to get myself round — she believes she is about to go on stage to present a special edition of her television show here for charity — and I think I can just, good-afternoon.
Jude (*as Fay*) Oh my God, it's you! You're not here for *me*, are you. It can't be me!
Gillian Fay Finch — *This is Your Life!*
Jude I felt so proud of you!
Gillian You knew, didn't you. You were expecting it. Admit it, you'd worked it out.

Jude She didn't. Did you know, Fay? Of course she didn't.

Fay covers her head with a cushion

Fay Don't speak to me. I don't want anyone to speak to me.
Gillian I give up.
Jude Fay. Darling. Let me at least get you a cup of tea. Or would you rather have a drink?
Gillian She can't hear you.
Fay Why don't you both go away.

Jude stands looking anxiously down at Fay. She doesn't know what to do

Jude Oh. Dear.
Gillian (*taking off her coat*) I'd like a drink.
Jude We can hardly ——
Gillian Of course we can. Gin and tonic for me.
Fay Go away, the pair of you. Get out of my house.
Gillian Ice and lemon.

Jude hesitates a moment. Then she takes off her coat and opens the drinks cupboard

Jude I really thought she'd be pleased.
Gillian She is pleased.
Jude (*doubtful*) Do you think so? There's loads of gin but we seem to have run out of tonic.

Gillian looks in the drinks cupboard

Gillian I'll have a Scotch, then. As it comes.

During the following, Jude pours two Scotches. She gives one to Gillian who sits on a sofa. Jude then sits without a drink

Fay Go home the two of you and leave me to grieve alone.
Gillian They've done you a *This is Your Life,* for pity's sake, you've always wanted that and now you've got it — what's wrong with you?
Fay They made me look like a loser. A has-been. A barely-ever-was.
Gillian This is very wearing.
Jude How could you look like a loser, you're a household name, you've got your own show. How many people have their own show?
Gillian You looked fine.

Fay It was an obituary.
Jude You looked wonderful. You looked like a whole woman, a rounded human being.
Fay Who wants to look like a human being, we're all human beings. Even you. I needed to look like a star.
Gillian I don't know what more they could've done.
Fay They could've given me some razzmatazz, couldn't they? A bit of glitz, a bit of class. Why didn't you suggest people? You know who I know. You could at least have flown someone in, they always fly people in, I dunno — from L.A.
Gillian Well I'm sorry.
Fay You could've found me someone to sit next to. You wouldn't see Oprah sitting there all on her own. Well would you? You wouldn't see Ruby. Or, or Esther. They'd have a *loving partner* wouldn't they, in a chair right next to them. To gaze at them fondly and share private little jokes. And when they were moved to tears by the tributes from their friends, their extremely *famous* friends, they'd squeeze their hand.
Gillian A partner? You want a miracle? Michael took off decades ago.
Jude He'll be on location.
Gillian In some desert. With a thousand extras. And camels.
Jude And a megaphone. And his cap on back to front.
Gillian Anyway. He's been married twice since then.
Jude I thought it was three times.
Gillian He might bite your neck. I can't see him holding your hand.
Jude Would you want him to?
Fay Not Michael. Obviously not Michael. A friend.
Jude We thought of that. Gillian was keen to do it, weren't you Gilly? But they said it might've looked, you know, misleading.
Fay Someone famous. A famous friend.

Pause. Fay looks from one to the other

Oh, for goodness' sake. I have loads of famous friends. You know perfectly well. They come on the show all the time.
Jude They tried people, of course they did.
Gillian They tried a great many people.
Jude Everyone seems to be so busy.
Fay You could at least've got David. A son can sit next to his mother, can't he? A handsome and *famous* son. Why didn't you get David?

Pause

The shit.

Jude He had a big exhibition coming up.
Gillian He was on his way to Japan.
Jude His people faxed us.
Gillian They were hugely apologetic.
Jude It was a nice fax.
Fay The ungrateful little shit.
Gillian Oh come on, Fay. It wasn't so bad. The producer of your show was all right, wasn't he? I thought he was. That was a nice story he told.
Jude And the guy from the Consumers' Association wasn't bad. The tall one.
Gillian On the video link.
Jude With the bottle-glass specs.
Gillian That's right, *he'd* been on your show.
Jude He was good, wasn't he.
Gillian He was excellent.
Jude What's his name? He's quite well known.
Gillian You must've been pleased with him.

Fay sits up

Fay You had my father. For the *finale*.
Gillian He's such a character.
Jude And he's terribly proud of you.
Gillian And Richard Branson let us down.
Fay I feel completely humiliated.
Gillian Have a drink, you'll be fine. Jude. Give her a nice fat drink
Fay It was all so, so utterly daytime TV.
Gillian You are daytime TV.
Fay Damn you. Five-thirty is early evening.
Jude Here. (*She gives Fay her Scotch*)
Gillian Get that on board. (*Raising her glass to Fay*) Bottoms up, you ungrateful old bag.

Fay won't be mollified. But she does drink. Jude watches the others for a moment. Then she goes back to the drinks cupboard and pours one for herself

Jude Might as well. If that's OK. (*She rejoins the others on the sofas*) Well. This is nice, isn't it? Who wants to be at some glamorous celebrity party? With boring old smoked salmon sandwiches. And stupid old free champagne.

They drink in silence for a while

Gillian It was weird to see Miss Gillespie. Their researcher turned her up. I'd forgotten all about her.

Act I, Scene 1 5

Jude I hadn't. I dreaded double maths.
Gillian What a sadist. And she smelt of TCP. (*Pause*) Maybe there was too much of the early stuff. A bit. Early stuff is bound to be embarrassing. But those are the people it's easiest to get. They can't wait to see themselves up there, can they, early people. They're desperate for it.
Jude We're early people.
Gillian What?
Jude Well, we are. Old school friends. Not on the television or anything. We're early people.
Gillian Of course we're not. We're not, are we, Fay? We're not early, we're ongoing. You and her and me, we're lifelong friends.
Fay (*standing and taking off her coat*) Dump that for me, Jude. If you wouldn't mind. (*She kicks off her shoes*) And you might as well top this up (*her glass*) since you're on your feet. (*She sits again*)

Jude tidies away Fay's coat and pours her another drink during the following

I don't know. Maybe it might have been endurable. Livable down. Eventually. If it hadn't been for Bollards.
Gillian She was pretty frightful.
Fay She was excruciating.
Jude Poor old Bollards.
Gillian How can she have got like that?
Fay She was always like it.
Gillian I suppose she was. It was all so long ago.
Jude We were vile to her, weren't we? We were hateful to Bollards.
Fay Well, of course. It was impossible not to be.
Gillian She did kind of ask for it, didn't she?
Fay She was so spaniel-eyed. And adoring. And disgustingly eager to please.
Jude We encouraged it, though, we used her to show off to.
Fay She smelt of mothballs. And when she laughed, she *neighed*.

Gillian neighs

Jude We were horrible to her.
Fay Whatever possessed you to get Bollards?
Jude I don't know, really.
Gillian Did we ever discuss it?
Jude Didn't need to. She was just always on the list.
Gillian That's right, she was.
Jude Part of our lives, wasn't she?
Gillian A foregone conclusion.
Fay I think I could've borne it without Bollards.

There is a pause, while they all think back

Jude We shut her in the PE cupboard once, do you remember? And then we forgot and she stayed there all night.
Fay I expect she deserved it.
Jude We ran her pyjamas up the flagpole. She got grounded all term for that. They found her name tape in the trousers.
Gillian Did we have name tapes in our pyjamas?
Jude We had them in everything.
Fay I expect she was grateful for the attention.
Gillian She didn't go out much anyway.
Fay Weren't her parents divorced?
Jude Poor old Boll. She must've been wretched, mustn't she? She was always the one who got grounded.
Fay She was always the one who got caught.
Jude They expelled her in the end.
Gillian That wasn't our fault.
Jude Of course it was. Fay dared her to come on to Mr Hudson.
Gillian Mr "Name me the Great Lakes, now don't let me down girls, chop chop" Hudson.
Fay I didn't dare her to *sleep* with him.
Gillian "Go all the way."
Jude But you know how she was. She'd've wanted to impress you.
Gillian Getting pregnant was impressive.
Fay I'd've been a lot more impressed if they'd used a condom.
Jude Mr Hudson had to resign and I gave up Geography. He was quite good-looking, wasn't he? I rather fancied him myself.
Gillian You couldn't have done. He had kind of fawn hair on the back of his hands.
Jude D'you think they went through with it? And had the baby?
Gillian If Fay hadn't refused to go to the party, we might've found that out.
Fay I wouldn't be seen dead at a party with those people.
Gillian Jude had been looking forward to it, hadn't you, Jude?
Jude Can't think when I last went to a party. A baby Bollard. Can you imagine? Maybe Mr Hudson married her.
Gillian "Will you be my wedded wife, let's be having you, chop chop."
Jude I wish we'd been nicer to Bollards.

Gillian takes the big red book from the table and opens it

Gillian (*reading*) To my dearest Fay — This Is Her Life!
Fay Oh, no, don't, please don't.

Act I, Scene 1

Gillian In days so long past,
　　　　　She was top of our class,
　　　　　In Chemistry, Physics and French.
　　　　　With her plaits flying free,
　　　　　She would score one, two, three
　　　　　And never be left on the bench.
Fay Enough, enough!
Gillian She was head of the dorm
　　　　　And captain of form,
　　　　　In choir she could sing doh, ray, me,
　　　　　And I was so proud
　　　　　That out of the crowd
　　　　　My friend she had chosen to be.
Fay That's it now, no more!
Gillian And now she is grown,
　　　　　By all she is known,
　　　　　Her skills they are easy to number.
　　　　　She fights the good fight
　　　　　And puts our wrongs right
　　　　　Our foes they are all cast asunder.
Fay Oh God.
Gillian So with glasses held high,
　　　　　Let us joyfully cry,
　　　　　Three cheers for her courage and clout!
　　　　　Oh, hip-hip-hooray,
　　　　　We're so glad that you're Fay,
　　　　　You're the one we just can't do without!
Fay On primetime TV. How could you do that to me? I'll never live it down. Never.
Jude We weren't to know she'd write a poem.
Gillian Quite good, though, don't you think? I really like it.
Jude Sorry.

Jude catches Gillian's eye. They raise their glasses

　Hip-hip-hooray!
Gillian We're so glad that you're Fay ——
Jude　 ⎤
　　　　　 ⎥ *(together)* You're the one we just can't do without!
Gillian ⎦

They break up

Fay I hate you both. You've ruined my career. I hate you.

Gillian and Jude make a big effort and stop laughing. Fay suddenly grins

   She made her mark. You've got to hand it to her.
Gillian In a week, the horror will have faded.
Jude We've all come a long way since then.
Gillian A long, long way.
Jude It's almost like we're completely different people.
Gillian Thank God.
Jude Wiser people.
Gillian Quite successful people.
Jude Let's drink to the horror fading.
Fay Let's just drink.

The front doorbell rings

Fay Now what?
Gillian It's incredibly late.
Jude I'll go.
Fay We can't just open it.
Jude I don't mind.
Fay I'm a public figure. It could be anyone.
Gillian It'll be someone's minicab, won't it? Or their pizza.

The doorbell rings again

Jude I don't mind going.
Fay You stay where you are.
Gillian It could be some weirdo.
Fay The price we pay for celebrity. They'll go away.
Bollards (*off; as if through the letterbox*) Yoo–hoo!
Fay This really is too much.
Bollards (*off*) Coo-ee! Anybody ho-ome?

There is the sound of the door knocker

   (*Off*) Open up in the name of the Law-aw. Only joking!

Fay, Gillian and Jude realize who is outside

Gillian Oh no.
Jude How did she know where to come?

Act I, Scene 2

Fay Turn the light out.
Jude We can't do that. (*She moves towards the door*)
Fay I'll never forgive you for this. Never.

Black-out

SCENE 2

The same. Moments later

The Lights come up rapidly. Fay, Jude and Gillian are sitting on the sofas as before. Also on stage now are Bollards, still dressed in the new suit she bought for her television appearance, and her son, Allan

Bollards Do look at us all! I can barely believe I'm sitting here. In Fay Finch's actual house. Fay Finch. I think of you as that now. It's a much nicer name than Fay Fowler, isn't it. Your secret is safe with me. Oh it's beautiful, it's really beautiful. See that, Allan? That takes flair. I always tell people we were at school together, don't I? I get it in somehow. I was at school with Fay Finch. Gives me some cachet, doesn't it? In their eyes. Bit of an edge.
Jude It is very nice here.
Bollards Mind you. It's hard to find. I'm not blaming you, Gillian. But those directions you gave me were terribly vague. Even the number of the house was wrong. It's lucky for you I'm not that easily put off!
Gillian Careless of me.
Bollards I forgive you. No hard feelings. No harm done! We all get a bit scatty, don't we, as we get older. No point trying to hide our ages around here!
Jude Would you like something to drink, Bollards? How about you, Allan?
Bollards Oh Lord! Bollards! Everyone calls me Caroline these days, Judith.
Jude Scotch? Caroline?
Bollards I wouldn't say no.
Allan Do you have any Lucozade?
Bollards Allan has to be a wee bit careful. With his medication.
Jude Do we have —— ?
Fay Are you taking the piss?
Jude I'll see what I can find.

Jude exits to the kitchen

Gillian and Fay daren't meet each other's eye

Bollards I just can't believe I'm here.

Gillian It is quite hard to believe.

Bollards And what about you, Gillian? What are you up to these days? I hope you're not frightfully famous too. Showing my ignorance!

Fay Oh, I don't think you'd really be interested

Bollards I'm sure I would.

Fay She's a head-hunter.

Bollards Oh! Like in Borneo, d'you mean?

Fay She works in Executive Search.

Bollards Right. Well never mind, Gillian. We can't all be celebrities, can we?

Fay Bit of a success, though. Small firm of her own.

Gillian Not that small. Turnover couple of million a year.

Bollards Goodness. There must be a lot of lost executives.

Gillian This can't be happening.

Fay She's in recruitment. Tell her, Gilly.

Gillian You're a big City player OK, and you have a post to fill. You want the best man for the job, the best man in the world. But you probably don't know who that is. So. How're you going to go about getting him?

Bollards Haven't a clue. Not the foggiest.

Gillian That's the point, you see. No-one has. None of them has the foggiest so they have to call on me.

Bollards Good gracious!

Gillian That's the job. I have sources. I have contacts. I have intuition. And I'm very, very persuasive. I'll line up five of the best. Until my call they were happy where they were. Now all my City man has to do is choose between them.

Bollards And, don't tell me — he has to pay.

Fay It's a valuable service.

Gillian He's happy to pay.

Bollards That's marvellous.

Fay When she can pull it off, it is.

Bollards I just knew you lot were going to take the world by storm. I said as much to Miss Gillespie at the party. What happened to you at the party? Wonderful nibbles. Loads of champagne.

Gillian Something came up.

Fay We didn't quite make it.

Bollards What a shame. (*Pause*) And do you have an "S.O." Gillian?

Gillian A what?

Bollards Are you "with anyone"?

Gillian Ah.

Bollards A "significant other". I hope you don't mind me asking.

Gillian No. I don't mind your asking.

Pause

Act I, Scene 2   11

Bollards So. What about Judith? What's she up to? Something frightfully academic I bet. She always was the brainy one.

Jude enters with a glass for Bollards and Allan's drink — tomato juice — which she puts on the table

Gillian Well, here she is, she can tell you that herself.
Jude Is tomato juice OK? It's organic. Tell you what? (*She pours Bollards' Scotch during the following*)
Bollards He doesn't really care for vegetables.
Allan I don't like to think of them growing.
Bollards Gillian's just been explaining to us all about her employment agency, Judith. How about you?
Jude Oh. I don't really ... This and that. You know. Nothing exciting like them. I'm just, I'm gathering together some material. For a paper most probably. That sort of thing.
Bollards Research. You're so clever.
Jude On the Ancient Assyrians. Their manners and mores. I don't suppose anything'll come of it.
Bollards Oh, I'm sure it will. I think you've found a bit of a gap in the market there, Jude. No-one seems to talk much about Ancient Assyrians do they? Not these days.
Fay No-one I know.
Jude Actually it is quite interesting. Because although Assyria belonged to the kingdom of the Mitanni for ages and ages — we're talking Second Millennium BC here of course — it seems like Ashur its capital hung on to quite a bit of autonomy. And since it was so close to the boundary with Babylonia that meant it could play Babylonia off against the Mitanni all the time. So it's interesting. (*Pause*) Anyway.
Bollards I'd love to be brainy. I'm always saying that. Aren't I, Allan?
Jude Of course I don't have as much time to spend on it as I'd like. Because well there are always other things that seem to need doing.
Bollards We don't have to ask what *you're* up to, Fay. You've been keeping very quiet over there.
Fay Did you buy that outfit specially for your television debut?
Bollards I went to Harrods. Well. It was a special event. I'm glad you like it.
Fay I don't really.
Jude Fay. Don't start.
Bollards It's not really me, is it?
Fay It's not really anyone.
Bollards Oh. Oh well. I've never been much of a fashionista, I'm always saying that — aren't I, Allan?

Fay I wouldn't worry. It's not as though you'll be getting much wear out of it. You're not planning to broadcast any more of your *oeuvre*, are you? Unless of course they offer you Poet Laureate.

Bollards Well, of course I know they wouldn't do that. But I have had some of my efforts published, as it happens. In the church magazine.

Jude That's great, Boll. I'm soon going to be in a magazine too.

Bollards Are you, Judith? How exciting. Will it be about the Assyrians?

Jude No. It'll be about Fay. Because Fay's been asked to do the "Me and My Friend" feature. You know. Sunday supplement. Where they interview each of two old friends about the other. How they met and everything. And sometimes they're both famous, and sometimes only one of them is. And Fay's going to do it with me.

Bollards Aah. That's really lovely.

Jude I think it will be rather fun.

Gillian Actually she isn't.

Jude What?

Gillian She isn't doing it with you because she's doing it with me. Aren't you, Fay? You promised.

Fay Did I? I don't think I can have done that, Gilly. Not promised.

Gillian You did. You remember. I mentioned I was going through a quiet patch with the firm. (*To Bollards*) Nothing worrying of course. Temporary glitch. Happens all the time in business. (*Back to Fay*) And you asked, might the feature be helpful? And I said I thought it would. Well, it might. Something unexpected. A little reminder for people. At least it couldn't do any harm. And you said right, you'd see what you could do.

Fay Exactly.

Gillian Well. "See what you could do." You don't actually have to "see what you can do." It's up to you, isn't it?

Fay Exactly.

Jude Fay's giving it to me because of the wedding, Gilly. I'm so sorry. I'd like to say you could have it instead, I mean I wouldn't normally care. But you know how it is. It's Julie's wedding next month. And Denis will be there with bloody Lavinia. And you know how he always makes out I'm so hopeless at everything. And I've put on a bit of weight recently and she's so stick thin. And the feature, well the feature'll make it that much easier, won't it. Less of an ordeal. If everyone's just read about me, you know, in the colour supplement. Sorry Gilly. But that's why she's giving it to me.

Gillian Are you giving it to her?

Fay I may have said it was an option.

Jude It was a bit more definite than that.

Fay One of several possible options.

Jude I see.

Fay And as of tonight. After this unexpected celebration of my career. I've started to firm up my strategy. *Vis-à-vis*, "Me and My Friend".

Act I, Scene 2   13

Jude Oh.
Fay I've decided to go for a more A-list kind of chum. You know the sort of thing. Celebrity presenter, Fay Finch, with her sparkling celebrity friendship. Rather than Fame-never-changed-her Fay Finch with her Surprisingly Ordinary Old Mucker.
Jude Right.
Gillian Damn you, Fay.
Bollards Fame-never-changed-her Fay *Fowler* that would be. Presumably. Only joking.

Pause

Allan I don't mind the occasional potato.

Pause

Bollards Is Julie your daughter, Judith? Lovely for you she's getting married.
Jude What? Oh yes. I suppose it is. She's still so young. I hope she won't regret it. (*To Fay*) It would make such a difference, Fay.
Fay Well, there it is. Too bad. It can't be helped.

Pause. Jude turns back to Bollards

Jude I'm sorry. Yes, you're right, it is lovely.
Bollards I married very young myself, of course.
Jude Did you? I mean we had rather been wondering. Did you marry Mr Hudson?
Bollards Yes, I did. I married him.
Jude Well, Bollards! That's wonderful! Was it wonderful?
Bollards Oh, yes. Yes, of course. Very wonderful.
Jude He was rather good-looking, I always thought so. And not so terribly old, not really. And so Allan is ... Well, this is Allan!
Fay However did you manage to stop calling him Mr Hudson?
Bollards I never really have. Only kidding! But it was dreadfully hard to think of him as Brian. Just at first. Quite a little joke between us. Great one for a joke, Mr Hudson. You wouldn't've guessed that, would you, from Geography. No. Fantastically big on jokes. In the joke, he's still Mr Hudson the teacher and I'm still the silly little schoolgirl. Who has no idea where Burkino Faso is.
Gillian Or the Great Lakes, "don't let me down now girls, chop chop"!
Bollards That's it. You've got it. Jokes all the time, hey, Allan? Loads and loads of jokes.
Jude Did he get another job all right? After he, you know ——?

Bollards Yes. Oh, yes, he did, thanks for asking. He did. Not teaching Geography of course, not in a school. Well, because of that whole silly references palaver. And everything. But English as a Foreign Language — you know, to overseas students — nothing at all to be ashamed of in that.
Jude Certainly not.
Bollards A bit frustrating at first, probably. Which at times he couldn't help taking out on me. But that's understandable, isn't it? I think so. And of course I understood. But to answer your question, yes, wonderful. Very well-suited, tremendously well, undoubtedly. In the circumstances that prevailed. So. Wonderful is what it was.

Pause

Gillian And what about you? Did you have work of your own?
Fay Or were you just a housewife?
Bollards I was only sixteen. No qualifications. And a brand new baby. It was all a bit ——
Gillian Much?
Bollards Yes. A bit ——
Jude Overwhelming.
Bollards (*suddenly standing*) I wonder if I might possibly. Have another drink?

Jude and Gillian both stand. Gillian takes Bollards' glass over to the drinks cupboard and pours drinks for herself and Bollards. Jude and Bollards sit down again. Pause

I can't've been too bad as a mother, though. I must've been doing something right. Because Allan's still living at home, aren't you, Allan?
Jude I wish we'd been nicer to you at school, Bollards.
Bollards Oh. Well, you have to be able to take a joke, don't you? That's one of Mr Hudson's. You have to be able to take a joke.

Gillian brings Bollards her drink and one for herself. Fay hands over her glass, Gillian picks up Jude's too and takes them over for refills

Gillian More Scotch, girls, chop chop.
Bollards I went to night school later, though. Picked up a few O's and A's. This and that. And now I'm on the local council.
Jude You've done brilliantly, Bollards.
Bollards I haven't done badly, have I? Sometimes, before I fall asleep at night, I do wonder what might've happened, if things had started out differently. I wasn't such a bad student, was I? Not brainy like Judith. Or

Act I, Scene 2   15

lively like Gillian. Or a born leader like Fay. But I maybe could have done something.
Jude What would you like to've done?
Bollards Oh, I don't know. It's all a bit silly, really, thinking about it. But I'd've liked to be famous like Fay. All sorts of people start out normal and get famous these days, don't they? I'd've liked that. I felt a bit famous tonight, tell you the truth. Standing up there in front of the cameras, and everyone could see Fay Finch was my friend. You can tell people, can't you, till you're blue in the face but you catch them with a funny little smile, you know, they get that "oh yeah" look in their eye. But now they'll have to believe me. Because I've been on the television. Of course being on the television for knowing someone else isn't the same as being on it in your own right. I know that. Yeah. So that's what I'd like to've done. I'd've liked to've been on the television in my own right.

Gilly rejoins them and hands Jude and Fay their drinks

Gillian Skin off your nose, girls.
Fay Maybe being on the television isn't all it's cracked up to be.
Bollards It's very nice of you to say that, Fay. I appreciate it. But I'd like Allan to be proud of me.
Jude I'm sure Allan's already proud of you. (*Pause*) Aren't you, Allan?
Allan Yeah.
Jude And I'm sure Mr Hudson's proud of you too. What a pity you didn't bring him along with you tonight. It would've been fascinating to meet him again. Wouldn't it, girls? After all these years.
Bollards Well to tell you the truth I don't think tonight would have been quite exactly a Mr Hudson kind of evening.

Allan gets to his feet, knocking over his untouched tomato juice. A wide red stain travels fast over the glass table and begins to run on to the rug

Jude and Gillian leap up

Bollards Allan, I do wish you'd be more careful!
Gillian Cloth. Towel. Salt.

Jude and Gillian head for the kitchen. Bollards makes to stand up

Jude It's fine. No, Bollards, stay where you are.
Bollards I'm so sorry, the rug, your beautiful rug.
Jude It'll all be perfectly fine.

Gillian and Jude exit and return with cloths and a container of salt

They clean up the mess. Allan shifts and hovers and flaps his arms like a wading bird in distress. Only Fay is unmoved. Gradually calm is restored. All but Jude sit down again. Jude pours a thick layer of salt over the remaining mark on the rug

There we are. By morning, no-one'll know it's there. (*She sits down too*)

Pause

Bollards In addition to which. Mr Hudson has, quite some time ago in fact. Unfortunately died.

Black-out

Scene 3

The same. A little later

The Lights come up rapidly. Fay and Gillian are alone on the sofas

Fay God, I'm tired. What a nightmare. D'you think she'll ever go?
Gillian She's not that bad. Poor old thing. She's better than I remembered her.
Fay She'll be a whole lot better without that suit.
Gillian Are you really going to let her take whatever she wants?
Fay She has the run of my wardrobe.
Gillian That's a bit rash. Jude's upset with you. She'll point her towards the good stuff.
Fay Jude has no idea what's good.
Gillian She knows what's expensive.

Pause

Fay *This Is Your Life*. After all these years. I had sussed it.
Gillian I knew you had.
Fay I couldn't help it. I heard Jude on the phone.
Gillian Why didn't you put a stop to it. If you didn't want it.
Fay I didn't want it.
Gillian Well, then.
Fay I was banking on it. To make me look — incomparable. You know, irreplaceable. An institution. I needed to look ahead of the game and at the top of my field.
Gillian You are all those things. You know you are.

Fay But I didn't look it.
Gillian What can I say. Sorry.

Pause

Fay They may be going to axe the show.
Gillian I suppose it's about time, really. Ever since Eamonn Andrews. Who's left to do? It's run its course.
Fay *My* show.
Gillian What? Of course they're not. Are you sure?
Fay We're not essential viewing any more.
Gillian People love you.
Fay No, they don't. They're just — used to me.
Gillian They want what you do.
Fay Yeah. And they want someone young doing it.
Gillian You've got weight. You've got wisdom. You've got maturity.
Fay Mature is a bad age for a woman.
Gillian They can't do that to you.
Fay They can do it to anyone. I'm so scared, Gilly. I can't sleep and I can't think. Each day I go in, I'm expecting the sword to fall.
Gillian What'll happen to you?
Fay I shall become ordinary. I was ordinary before and I shall revert.
Gillian Oh, Fay. It's not definite, is it? What would it take to turn things round?
Fay A bloody miracle.

Allan comes trailing in from the stairs

Ah. News from the Front.
Gillian Any luck? Found her something?

Allan sits

Allan She's trying on totally everything.
Gillian That's my girl.
Allan I've never seen so much stuff.
Fay It's getting rather late.
Allan You have a lorry-load of gear up there, Ms Finch.
Gillian We were sorry to hear about your father, Allan. It must've been a very great loss.

Allan shifts. Bollards' neigh comes floating down the stairs

They seem to be enjoying themselves.

Allan She never gets to wear nice clothes.
Fay Is that so? It's been a long time since we've seen your mother.
Gillian Such a pity. But we didn't keep in touch.
Fay You know how it is. We'd no means of knowing where she was.
Allan She knew where you were.
Fay Ah well, yes.
Allan But then, stands to reason, live in the studio each week, everybody knows where you are.
Fay There's bound to be a certain one-sidedness. In my sort of work.
Allan Majorly unpleasant I'd call that, Ms Finch. I'd call it gross.
Fay Oh, I wouldn't say that. It doesn't seem gross to me, Allan. Because I'm used to it.
Allan If a friend loses touch with my mother, it's because they've mislaid her address. If they lose touch with you though, it's because they choose to.
Fay Ah well. When it comes to friends. One tends to seek out one's own level.

Pause

Gillian What's your line of business, Allan?
Allan My business?
Gillian Your job.

Pause

I didn't mean to pry. People are generally happy to talk about their work. I am. I enjoy talking about it.
Allan Your work that's going through the quiet patch, you mean? That's in the temporary glitch?

Gillian rises

Gillian Can I get anyone another drink?

Fay hands over her glass; Gillian pours more drinks

Allan I thought you were asking about my job. Don't have a job. Applied for one or two but didn't get them. I'm not thought suitable for jobs. I don't mind talking about my work though.
Fay Feel free.
Allan I make car-sized versions of Dinky Toys. Takes me a year to do one at present but I think I'll get faster. I've made nine so far, including the

Act I, Scene 3   19

boxes. I've just completed a number 158, Riley Saloon, plum red, with opening doors, bonnet and boot.
Gillian Splendid.
Fay But aren't Dinky Toys already miniature versions of cars?
Allan That's the beauty of it.

Gillian comes back with the drinks

Gillian They don't *go* then?
Allan Of course not. Dinky cars don't go. The essence of the Dinky, if you think about it, Gillian, is, number one: verisimilitude, number two: the hand, number three: the brrm-brrm-brrm. I capture the verisimilitude, yeah? And whoever comes to view provides the hand.
Fay Fascinating.
Gillian There's a soundtrack of some sort running then, is there? I'm assuming. To give you some number three.
Allan Haven't you ever played with a Dinky Toy, Ms. Finch? It's the owner of the hand's responsibility to come up with the brrm-brrm-brrm.
Gillian Right.
Fay They must take up a lot of space.
Allan I store them in a disused warehouse in Sydenham. And my mother lets me work on the current model at home.
Gillian That's very tolerant of her.
Allan She likes the company.

Bollards' laughter comes down from upstairs

Fay They surely can't be going to take much longer.
Allan Dinky Toys themselves, of course, have become collectors' items. Quite ordinary cars routinely fetch a hundred pounds at sales. And a very rare one, in pristine condition, with box, could go for a cool three thou.
Gillian Do you have much of a collection yourself, Allan?
Allan Oh yeah. Cupboardsful. (*He turns out half a dozen from his pockets on to the coffee table*) But I'd never sell them, not at any price, not to anyone, so they can't be reckoned an investment.

Fay stands up

Fay I'll have to call them.
Allan Oh don't do that. It would be kinder not to. My mother's had so little pleasure since she killed my father.

Fay and Gillian round on him in disbelief

Bollards enters from the stairs with a great flourish, in a dark purple kaftan, gold around the neck. Jude follows behind her

Bollards Da *ner!* This is the one, girls. It becomes me, don't you think. This is the gown you were wearing, Fay, to present your show about Grief.

Black-out

SCENE 4

The same. Moments later

The Lights come up rapidly. Fay, Gillian, Jude and Allan are seated. Bollards is modelling the gown, posing, parading, turning, dancing. She's excited by it; she feels like Fay, it's given her confidence. Fay and Gillian still stunned, Allan nonchalant, Jude oblivious

Bollards You were wearing this dress and you looked wonderful. I was so proud of you. Fay Finch. My childhood friend. And you said, "There are many experiences in life it's possible to imagine, even if we haven't lived through them ourselves. But there are others. Others we may think we can imagine, but which are in fact so unlike anything else we have to go on, that our conjurings can only be woefully inadequate. Dying is one of these. Childbirth is another. And a third is loss of a loved one. Look around you. Look at the person beside you. Behind you. No-one in the studio here tonight, ladies and gentlemen, has to struggle to imagine what this last experience might feel like because they have all felt it themselves. Are feeling it right now. And will continue to feel it to some degree for the whole of the rest of their lives."

Jude applauds

Jude That's wonderful, Bollards. You sound just like her.
Bollards Do I, do I really? I still get a shiver right through me when I think of you saying that, Fay. "And continue to feel it to some degree for the whole of the rest of their lives." That is just so true. That is one of the truest things I ever heard. And you know what is specially wonderful about the way you said it? You made us all think you were one of the people who didn't have to try to imagine it. Even though, as it later turned out, you were one of the people who did. You've never lost a loved one.
Fay Well, I ——
Bollards When Mr Hudson died we'd been married fifteen years. I was still only thirty-one. He'd been my constant companion, my mainstay and my

Act I, Scene 4

mentor, all my adult life. I didn't have to imagine anything, Fay. And yet you who did, made me feel you understood. Not only understood. Understood better than I.
Allan Sit down, Mum.
Bollards I love this dress. This is a magician's dress. It gives me strength. It gives me presence. It gives me power.
Jude She can have it if she likes it, can't she, Fay? You said she could choose.
Bollards I love, I love, I love this dress!
Jude Fay?
Fay She can have it.
Bollards Can I? Can I really? Really, really have it?
Fay I said so, didn't I?
Gillian Boll.
Bollards Thank you so much. Thank you, thank you, thank you.
Gillian Bollards.
Bollards Tonight I am the luckiest woman in this entire world. The whole wide world.
Gillian How did Mr Hudson die?

Bollards stops twirling and spinning and dancing

How did he?
Jude Gilly, that's ... Maybe Bollards doesn't want to talk about that now. Maybe Allan——
Gillian I want to know how he died.

Pause

Bollards (*dreamy*) Mr Hudson was a very clever man. He knew everything. Not just about Geography, where every country in the world was, what its capital was, annual rainfall, beef exports and gross national product. But everything about everything. The distance from here to the planet Mercury. Margot Fonteyn's real name. The way to tell the difference between a rook and a crow, what egregious means, why the washing machine is making that funny noise, what String Theory is and the best way to get to Birmingham without using the motorway.
Fay I'll ring for a cab. You can come back for the car in the morning.
Allan Don't worry about it. I can look after her.
Bollards I'm not going home. I like it here. I like wearing this dress. Where could I ever wear a dress like this but here?
Jude (*to Gillian*) Are you out of your mind? (*To Bollards*) Sit down, Boll. Just sit there quietly.

Bollards sits

There now. And what line of business are you in, Allan?
Fay He makes big Dinky cars. (*To Bollards*) Wouldn't you like me to get you a cab?
Bollards (*wondering at it*) One of the things a person who has not experienced loss may find hard to imagine. May not even get as far as to imagine that they should be trying to imagine. Is that it's possible to be quite overwhelmed by grief for a person one thought one scarcely loved at all.
Allan Would you like to hold the Sunbeam Talbot, Mum. It's your favourite. (*He gives her one of the little cars from the table*)

Bollards turns the car over and over in her hands

Bollards Mr Hudson died. In a motor vehicle accident.
Jude How terrible for you both. That must've been quite, quite terrible. (*She darts an accusing look at Gillian*) Now. How about I make everyone a cup of tea. D'you have any milk, Fay? Before we all go home.
Bollards (*lost in her own world*) It was a beautiful day. Autumn. Windy. Leaves gusting down the street. You know, that light metallic scrape. I was to drive Allan to his oboe class. Mr Hudson studied oboe from a very young age and never had cause to regret it. The car was in the garage.
Allan Two door Morris Traveller, Lincoln Green.
Bollards Garage, to gate, to roadway. It's an odd angle. Bit of a slope. Tricky manoeuvre. Scraped the wing quite badly once but that was years before. Used to it now, did it all the time, did it every single day. But Mr Hudson didn't quite trust me.
Allan Brrm. Brrm, brrm.
Bollards He'd come home early. Did I mention that it was a very beautiful day? He watched while I opened the garage. And then he stood by the wall like a traffic cop. I can do it, I said. I do it all the time on my own. But he went on standing there. You couldn't stop him doing a thing, not once he'd started, it was a point of principle with him. And he said, "Brake off, clutch down, put her into gear now, easy, easy, steady does it, back, back, back, and hold it. Now left hand hard down, left, left, left, left, *left*."
Jude Oh my God. Oh no.
Bollards I don't know why he said left. He should've said right. Mr Hudson was a man who knew everything.

There is a long silence

Fay Bollards?

Bollards slowly turns and looks at her

Act I, Scene 5

How would you like to appear on my show?

A moment

Black-out

Scene 5

The set of "Frankly Fay"

Big show music plays

The Lights come up brightly. Fay's empty sofas are now doing duty as the set of her TV show

Fay, presenting, stands in front of the sofas

The music ends and there is loud applause

Fay This evening I want to introduce those of you here in the studio, and all of you watching at home, to a very extraordinary woman. We have explored many tough subjects together in the years *Frankly Fay* has been on air, but never I believe one as painful as this. I ask you now to open your hearts, lay judgement aside and listen to her story. Try and imagine what she must have suffered, this patient, docile, loving mother of one, since that tragic day, not too long ago, when on a quiet suburban street, in a town just like yours, she came face to face with her nightmare. The horror that she, and she alone, had at that very moment, killed her own dear husband. It is my privilege to welcome here tonight, the honest, the courageous, the *amazing,* Caroline Pollard!

Bollards walks out into the light

The sound cuts out

Black-out

ACT II

Scene 1

Fay's sitting room Several weeks later

Bollards is hoovering, with obvious pleasure, wearing what Fay was wearing in Act I

Jude enters through the main door with her bag and stands watching. Bollards sees her and is startled

Bollards Aaah! Oh, you really … You can't hear a thing when you're hoovering, can you? Like the shower scene. (*She does the "Psycho" "Deep, deep, deep, deep" and stabs the air violently*) Anyone could come in and … And you'd never know.
Jude At least you'd have your clothes on.
Bollards That's some comfort.

Jude drops her bag on a chair and throws her coat down

Bollards I've just tidied up in here.
Jude Actually. You seem to have *Fay's* clothes on.
Bollards Yes … I … yes. I know. It's such a beautiful house. Be a shame to let it down, well wouldn't it, I think it would, with my old chain store stuff. How did you get in?
Jude I have a key.
Bollards Do you? How lovely.

Jude parks herself on a sofa and eyes Bollards curiously

Jude Does she know you're here?
Bollards Of course she does, my goodness me!

Jude continues to eye her

> Well, not exactly. She knows I came. With Allan. But she doesn't know I haven't gone.

Act II, Scene 1 25

Jude Allan's here?
Bollards He's in the garage. Making a life size replica of the Dinky model of Fay's car. He likes Fay's car. Fay thinks he's talented. She says it'll be an artwork when it's finished and very valuable, what with the box and everything, the way he does them. But Allan says he'll never sell, he makes them for love. He wasn't going to come at all but she told him it was a double one. The garage. There's not much room for him at home.
Jude You were hoovering.
Bollards I know. The rug comes up lovely, doesn't it?

Bollards wraps the cord round the hoover and takes it out to the kitchen

The cordless phone starts to ring. Jude rises to answer it. Before she can get to it, it stops. She goes back to her bag and gets out a sheaf of typed letters and envelopes

Bollards returns

Bollards They thought I was Fay. Can you believe that? That is so incredible! Oh, I didn't *say* I was, I'm not that bad — but I didn't exactly say I wasn't either. We had this whole conversation. You think they'd know she couldn't be here, I mean, really, when it's a studio day.
Jude You answered the phone?
Bollards I know. Amazing, isn't it?
Jude Yeah.
Bollards Coupla months ago I'd've never done a thing like that. Can you imagine? But since I did the show, it's like I'm — in the same business.
Jude Who was it?
Bollards Oh, just some bloke offering her a commercial. I said no. Fay doesn't do commercials.
Jude I'm not sure Fay'd want you answering her phone.
Bollards Oh c'mon. What're we going to do? Stand around like lemons and let it ring?
Jude I would've answered it myself.

Pause

Bollards I find that just a teensy bit offensive, Judith. If you don't mind me saying.
Jude I just meant I'd be a lot more likely to ——
Bollards I know what you meant.
Jude I don't think you do.
Bollards You think I'm a loser. Not up to answering someone's phone. And you despise me for going on Fay's show.

Jude Of course I ——

Bollards It was weeks and weeks ago and you've never said a single thing about it. You've never said, "Good for you, you did brilliantly." Or "What a funky thing to do."

Jude It's not that I despise you.

Bollards My friends at home all sent me cards. I got loads of them. All the tabloids picked it up. *Heat* and *OK* called me "dignified" and "moving". There was a three page spread in *Woman's Own*. People responded, they really did, they were interested. You could at least be pleased for me. Even Gillian texted.

Jude I am pleased. If it's what you want. I really, really am. It's true I should've ... Well done on the show. And — and the magazines. Well done you.

Bollards I've had loads of fantastic feedback.

Jude Have you?

Bollards Loads.

Jude Well that's good, isn't it?

Bollards The women especially, they really seem to respond to me.

Jude The ones who wish their husbands dead, presumably. No. I didn't mean — I'm sorry.

Bollards You don't get it, do you. They stop me in the street. A woman came up to me yesterday. I was at the checkout in Tescos. Just standing there. Four chicken thighs and a packet of pasta twirls. No make-up or anything. She said she could see my anguish.

Jude Boll ...

Bollards She thought I was very close to God.

Jude Bollards ——

Bollards I really would prefer you to call me Caroline. Especially now, you know?

Jude Are you quite certain you want to get sucked into all this? You don't have to go on with it.

Bollards What're you talking about?

Jude It was a terrible thing that happened to you. It's very personal stuff you're trading in.

Bollards Trading! I'm sure you don't mean to be hurtful, Judith. But I didn't get paid a penny for doing *Frankly Fay*. And there are other avenues opening up, that have nothing to do with "the terrible thing", almost nothing, which I'm not at liberty to talk about just at the moment.

Jude What other things?

Bollards I don't suppose anything will come of it. But the word from the Fifth Floor is, they like me. I'm more than usually ordinary is the thing. Oh, laugh if you want. It may seem easy to you, to, to look ordinary up there on the television. But there's a lot of lights you know, and people with

Act II, Scene 1

clipboards, and it takes a certain ... well, if it's something they think I can do I'm not going to argue with that.

Jude I'm not really laughing. And I thought you were very — courageous. To talk about such an awful thing. In front of millions of people.

Bollards Did you?

Jude I know it must have been difficult for you.

Bollards Yes, it was. But only at first. When I walked out on to that set I thought I would die. Of the embarrassment and the shame. Of, of the exposure. But once I started to talk, and I could hear their silence, and feel them listening, really listening. To *me*. Well, then I wished it would go on forever. I felt more significant than I've ever felt before. I felt powerful. I felt like a star. I felt, I really did, I felt — like Fay.

Jude But you could still — extricate yourself. People have very short memories.

Bollards Thank you for your concern, Judith. But I'm perfectly happy with the way things are.

Pause

Jude I can hardly blame you. This is all our fault. Can you ever forgive us?

Bollards What for?

Jude You know what for. For, oh, for all of it. We must have made you desperately unhappy.

Bollards I really don't remember.

Jude You do. I know you do.

Bollards What is it you want from me, Judith. Absolution?

Jude I'm so sorry. We were just children. We didn't know. But we're grown women now and we don't have to prove things to each other.

Bollards We're women but you're all up there, aren't you? Meeting people and doing stuff. Being wonderful. And look at me. It's the same. It's all still the same. You're not going to talk me out of it. I want this.

Jude Oh Boll. We all have our difficulties.

Bollards Gillian's glamorous and successful. You're a distinguished academic. And Fay's a household name.

Jude Maybe it's not quite exactly how we might've made it sound.

Bollards You're all the bee's bloody knees and what am I? I've run over my husband.

Jude Nobody thinks ——

Bollards Nothing at all has changed and that's what I can't forgive.

Pause

Difficulties?

Jude Oh, well. You know.
Bollards What difficulties?
Jude It doesn't matter exactly what. I just don't want you wasting your whole life feeling *less*. You're as good as anyone. Don't envy us.
Bollards Your marriage broke up. Tough. Gillian's business had a slow year. I'm sorry. You call those difficulties? I do envy you.
Jude It's never how it looks, of course it's not. Take me, for instance.
Bollards What about you?
Jude Nothing we have to go into. It isn't really anything. But I'm maybe not as successful as I seem.
Bollards Aren't you?
Jude No.

Pause. Jude doesn't elaborate

Bollards Well. It hardly matters. Whatever failures you think you've had, let's face it. You can't be less successful than me. There's hardly a soul on the face of the earth who's been less successful than me.
Jude Oh Boll. This is all so ... You know why I wanted to answer Fay's phone?
Bollards Because if I answered it, I'd be an embarrassment. And I was an embarrassment. I pretended to be Fay, for God's sake. They didn't just happen to think I was Fay, I pretended. I always do. I bring Allan as often as I can, Fay goes to the studio and I come in here and I pretend. It's an illness, isn't it? I know it's wrong. I've tried to give it up and I can't. I'm an embarrassment.
Jude Bollards.
Bollards Yes.
Jude I wanted to answer Fay's phone because — it's my job to answer it.
Bollards It's OK. You don't have to make me feel better. I'm kind of used to it now. I'm embarrassing.
Jude Listen to me, will you, just listen. Fay has a lot of money. I don't have any. She pays me. I pick up her mail, wait in for her parcels, deal with her bills, all the deadly stuff. I smooth the way for her. And when I'm here I answer her phone.
Bollards Fay employs you.
Jude Yes.
Bollards To do her menial tasks.
Jude Yes.
Bollards What about the Ancient Assyrians?
Jude Oh Boll. We all have to live.

Bollards embraces Jude warmly. Jude is awkward and uncomfortable. The phone rings. Neither of them moves to it. Bollards looks expectantly at Jude

Act II, Scene 2 29

> You answer it.
> **Bollards** Me? But shouldn't ——
> **Jude** That's OK, go on.

Bollards still hesitates

> Go on.

Bollards runs across the room and grabs the receiver

> **Bollards** (*as Fay, imperious, into the phone*) Yes. (*Longish pause*) Wait wait, hold on, this is most awfully tedious and dreary. I'll get my secretary to come and talk to you.

Black-out

Scene 2

The same. Soon afterwards

The Lights come up rapidly on Bollards and Jude, matey on the sofas. Allan is further away, on the floor, meticulously painting a flat section of his Dinky Toy box, paints and brushes beside him

> **Bollards** You were such an incredible brainbox, Judith. I simply can't imagine how it could've gone so wrong.
> **Jude** Oh well. That's because you never met Denis.
> **Bollards** Denis. Sounds quite reliable to me. Denis, Denis. Denis.
> **Jude** He was so beautiful. And so bright. Met him at a conference about prison reform. And I was working for the Home Office.
> **Bollards** You see.
> **Jude** And he was this high-flying lawyer. Speciality: Human Rights. Human Rights! Oh, a great one was Denis for the high moral ground.
> **Bollards** You're sounding just a wee bit bitter there, Judith.
> **Jude** I daresay I am. You know what they say, though. There's no-one more ruthless than an idealist.
> **Bollards** You must've loved him.
> **Jude** I adored him. Completely bowled over. I thought he was a shining hero. And Denis, well Denis found hero worship completely irresistible. He proposed to me on bended knee, at a rally for prisoners of conscience in Soviet Russia.
> **Bollards** Aah.
> **Jude** It was perfect at first. It really was. We had shared ideals and a comfortable house in Islington. A shiny car and two heavenly children, one

of each. I gave up my work to look after them when Denis explained that paying for childcare exploited women. He played around from the start, apparently. Gillian says he did. But I was too mesmerized to notice.
Bollards Oh, Judith.
Jude Maybe I shouldn't be saying all this in front of Allan.
Bollards Allan doesn't listen to anything, do you, pet? He's a man.

And he certainly doesn't react or look up. Pause

Something bad is going to happen, isn't it?
Jude Famine in Ethiopia happened. Fly-blown children too weak to stand or weep. Bob Geldof. Phil Collins. And the biggest rock music festival the world has ever seen.
Bollards Live Aid.
Jude Live Aid. And Denis rose up in a beautiful rage and said I will not live in luxury in Islington while children just the same as ours are dying right now for lack of a five pound sack of flour. And the next day, he traded in our shiny car. And took the children out of private school. And put our comfortable house on the market. And then he went round to the bank and pledged all the proceeds to Live Aid.
Bollards How amazing. Where were you supposed to live?
Jude At the same time he put down a payment on a medium-sized trailer in a trailer park in Dagenham East.
Bollards That is incredible. That is so ... Oh my God! You have to admit it's pretty impressive.
Jude Yes it was. I was impressed myself for a while. I might've been impressed for longer. If he hadn't moved out to live in a twenty-room castle in Scotland with a tobacco heiress, the spring of the following year.
Bollards No!
Jude Leaving me in the trailer in Dagenham with two small kids, a first-class degree in Middle Eastern History and no income.
Bollards Oh Judith. What, what a total catastrophe. Poor, poor you.
Jude (*standing suddenly*) Sorry. Sorry. I can't stand people being nice to me. I should never've ... Let's do something. What shall we do? How about a bit of hoovering?
Bollards It's OK. Sshh. Sit down. Relax. Just tell me everything that happened. Sometimes we need that.
Jude Nothing at all happened. I had a complete nervous collapse. I failed to cope. I failed to get up. I failed to do anything at all. If Fay hadn't paid me to collect her dry cleaning, my children would have gone into care and I'd be dead in the gutter by now.
Bollards It was a tough one, Judith, a really tough one. And secretarial work is a perfectly respectable ——

Act II, Scene 2   31

Jude It was twenty years ago, Boll. The children have grown. My friends have careers. There are new and greater famines in Africa. The world has turned. The world has turned, but I'm still there.
Bollards Still there? Where? Not in the trailer park. You're not still living in the trailer?
Jude Why are we talking about this? I never talk about it. Not to Fay, not to Gilly, not to anyone. I don't want to talk about it! (*She stares accusingly at Bollards*)

Bollards struggles to regain her composure. She stands

Bollards I'm going to make us all a cup of tea.

Bollards exits towards the kitchen

Jude watches her go

Jude Oh why did I say all that, why? How did I let that happen?
Allan (*without looking up from his work*) That's just what our vicar said. After he'd told her he had recurrent dreams about the curate.
Jude You do listen.
Allan Those who don't appear to listen, do frequently hear. Others, straining for each word, miss everything.
Jude God, you're annoying.
Allan So I've been told.
Jude Your father was annoying too.

This does make Allan look up

God rest his soul. (*She moves towards a paint brush*) Can I fill in a bit of red? It's years since I've done anything like this.

Allan gathers the brushes to safety and scrambles to his feet, standing over the box like an animal guarding its young

Allan Don't... I don't... No, don't, don't. You mustn't touch it. (*He watches her balefully during the following*)
Jude (*backing off*) All right, calm down. It was just a passing fancy. I'm hardly going to wrestle you to the ground for it, am I? Inflict Grievous Bodily Colouring-in. (*She flings herself back on the sofa*) God, I'm depressed. (*Pause*) Oh get on with your box, why don't you? Just pretend I'm not here — that shouldn't be hard, everyone else does.

Allan moves towards Jude. It feels a little menacing

Allan You're never going to make anything of yourself, not now.
Jude I daresay you're right, Allan.
Allan You're too highly qualified in a narrow field without any practical application.
Jude I don't need you to ——
Allan You are of no value at all to the Fifth Floor. My mother, on the other hand, knows very little about anything and as such is full of potential. She is a *tabula rasa* for them to scrawl across.
Jude Oh, really.
Allan The Fifth Floor is grooming my mother. (*Pause*) Maybe you don't believe me?
Jude It's not that I don't believe you ——
Allan That's why they're making Ms Finch bring her back on to *Frankly Fay*.
Jude What?
Allan They've insisted upon it. Ten minutes to show what she can do, next Friday.

Bollards enters with a tray of tea and an elegant deli pastry

Bollards Are you joining us, pet? Found this in the fridge. I don't think Fay'd begrudge us each a teeny slice, do you?

Black-out

Scene 3

The same. That night

The Lights come up rapidly on Fay, Jude and Gillian. Jude and Gillian have coats and bags with them

Gillian You must not allow this. Promise me you won't allow it.
Fay It's not up to me.
Gillian It's your show. It's been your show for fifteen years. Tell her, Jude.
Fay I'm not in a very strong position. We're haemorrhaging ratings. The Open University gets more than us.
Gillian There must be a better ratings pull than Bollards!
Fay There's a lot of interest out there in Bollards.
Gillian Interest? In Bollards? You can't be serious.
Jude She's a nice enough woman, Fay. But she's only one story to tell.
Gillian It'll go to her head. They'll make a monster of her.
Jude She is rather lapping it up.

Act II, Scene 3   33

Gillian And then when it's over. In about two weeks. She'll be a basket case.
Jude And we'll be the ones who're stuck with her. Oh dear. That's not very nice, is it? I don't mean stuck.
Gillian We will though. We'll never be rid of her now.
Jude Surely you can use your veto, Fay.
Gillian I can't believe you'd let them walk all over you.
Fay Fact is girls, I'll last as long as I can draw an audience. Not one day longer. If Bollards can revive my ratings, she'll be doing me a favour.
Jude They were all over you a few years back.
Fay They're not sentimental. Get me a drink will you, Jude. And let's talk about something else.

Jude sorts out drinks and they settle into the sofas

Jude Well. One Friday. Ten minutes. It's not that long. We'll get over it.
Gillian She was a complete nonentity before. She'll be a complete nonentity again.
Jude We can all change our phone numbers.
Gillian Fay'll have to move of course.
Jude But that'll be a small price to pay.
Gillian It'll be as though it never happened.
Jude Like some horrible dream.
Gillian Like your marriage to Denis.
Jude Like childhood.
Fay For Pete's sake, you two. *Stop talking about it!*
Jude Sorry. We were only trying to cheer you up.
Gillian Cheer ourselves up.
Jude Ten minutes, Fay. It's really not that long.
Fay It could well be every Friday. If they like what she does.
Gillian What?
Fay It could be a regular feature.
Gillian This has to be a joke.
Fay They think they're on to something. Mrs Everywoman. Mrs "However mundane you are at home, you're no more mundane than this".
Jude Oh, Fay.
Fay She won't challenge anyone. She won't make them feel small or stupid or insignificant. It's what they want.
Gillian You know what. It could happen. It really could. Bollards could be massive. Oh God. I'm having a panic attack. What's *wrong* with us? Can you imagine, when we were fifteen, we'd have let it get this far?
Fay Get a grip, Gilly. We're not fifteen.
Gillian You're the worst. You've totally given up. You're just — letting it happen. Are you really going to let Bollards get famous?

Jude It would be quite hard to take, if Bollards got famous.
Fay Well. It may be something we have to come to terms with.
Gillian (*leaping to her feet*) I shall never come to terms with it. And neither must you. If you can't sway the Fifth Floor, we must take her out of the running.
Jude Take her out?
Fay Back the car out of the garage and run her over in the drive?
Jude She doesn't mean that — you don't, do you, Gilly?
Gillian We need to sit her down and talk to her. Explain what daytime celebrity really costs. What it does to you, deep inside. Week in week out. On some trashy little show for the entertainment of morons.

Pause

Fay That's telling me.
Gillian Sorry. I take back trashy. But it's corrosive, you know it is. We all know. You're not the woman you were.
Fay Oh, I think I am, dear. I'm just not the woman I could have been.

Pause

Jude Erm. I don't think Bollards would be susceptible to that approach, Gilly.
Gillian What's wrong with it?
Jude The entertainment of morons is her ultimate goal in life.
Gillian OK. All right. If we can't appeal to Boll's better judgement, we shall have to appeal to Allan's. She might listen to Allan. Would you be prepared to talk to him?
Jude No.
Gillian No wonder you live in a van. You're always so totally negative.

Now Fay gets up

Fay Enough! I can't stand this! It's none of your business anyway. Go home the pair of you, and leave me in peace! (*She picks up Gillian's bag and shoves it at her*)
Jude (*standing*) It is quite late. Give me a call if you need me in the morning. (*She gathers up her jacket and puts it on*)
Gillian I didn't mean "trashy", Fay. You know I didn't.
Fay OK, OK.
Gillian I was just upset.
Fay OK.
Gillian (*moving towards the hall door*) C'mon Jude, I'll drive you home.

Act II, Scene 4   35

Jude (*still offended*) It's OK, I've got my bike.
Fay I'll be glad to see the back of you.

Gillian and Jude get to the door. Then Gillian freezes and turns

Gillian Hey! Eureka! Eureka! Euuuureka! (*She throws off her bag and pirouettes and sings the first line of "I Feel Pretty" from* West Side Story *wildly around the room*) Euur-frigging-reka! She's, she's got ten minutes on Friday, right. As a tryout. And if it doesn't go well she's finished. No second chance. We're not sentimental. One strike and you're out.
Jude But they're going to love her, aren't they?
Gillian No they're not, baby. No they are not. We don't have to mash her in the drive. Oh euuureka! All we have to do is help her!
Fay Are you insane?
Jude You're going to help her?
Gillian You bet I am. Kind, kind Gilly. I'm going to take her aside. And sit her down. And give her some sound advice. (*She puts her arms around each of the women*) Play safe, I'll say. Do what you're good at. We were all so impressed when we saw you on *This Is Your Life*. Just do what we know you're good at ...

Black-out

Scene 4

The set of "Frankly Fay"

Applause

The Lights come up on the sofas in show mode

Bollards stands in the glare of the lights. Gillian is in the background, watching on Fay's television

Silence falls. Very humbly, very brokenly, Bollards confides to the camera

Bollards In the glow of dawn,
           In the hush of night,
           My sleep is torn
           By grief and fright.

           I hear him call,
           I see him frown,

Oh why, oh why,
Said he, Left Hand Down?

So strong of limb,
So big of brain,
The sinister side
Destroyed my swain.

He was my love,
He was my mate,
But Left Hand Down
Has sealed our Fate.

Silence. Then massive and prolonged applause

Gillian Damn.

The Lights and applause fade

Scene 5

Fay's sitting-room

The Lights come up. There is a vase of flowers on the table. Gillian, at a loss, is standing in the middle of the room

Allan enters from the hall, his arms full of magazines, with a crate of his Dinky Toy collection on top

Gillian Allan!
Allan Brrm. Brrm.

Allan exits to the stairs

Bollards, in pinny and bandana, enters from the stairs with a pile of drying-up cloths and hot water bottles

Bollards Hiya!

Bollards exits into the kitchen

Gillian makes to follow her

Gillian Is Fay here?

Bollards enters from the kitchen with a mixer

Act II, Scene 5   37

Bollards We've got two of these now; I didn't know what to bring.
Gillian Where's Fay?
Bollards Upstairs in her bedroom, I think. Is something wrong?
Gillian I want to see Fay, that's all — does something have to be wrong? Is she resting?
Bollards Hiding, more likely. Expect she'll be down soon. Don't know what to do with this now.

Bollards exits into the kitchen

Allan enters from the stairs and exits into the hall

Gillian Hallo. (*Calling up the stairs*) Fay? It's Gilly. Can I come up and see you?

Bollards enters from the kitchen, kicks off her shoes, pulls off the pinny and bandana and flings herself on to the sofa, prostrate.

Bollards Give her a bit of a breather, I would. We're all exhausted.
Gillian I need to talk to her, it's nothing to do with you. (*But she comes away from the stairs*) What's going on?

Allan enters from the hall with another pile of things

Allan Brrm, brrm, brrm.

Allan exits to the stairs

Gillian You're not moving in, are you?
Bollards What an idea! We've just come to stay for a bit; makes sense. doesn't it? What with me doing the regular Friday slot and everything, and probably Wednesdays too — get me! Did you hear about that? — we can talk stuff through, and — have meetings. Speeds things up and that, saves on the phone bill! And I can do Fay's letters for her.
Gillian Jude does Fay's letters.
Bollards I know. She'll be pleased, won't she? She needs the time. For her Assyrians.
Gillian Did Fay invite you here?
Bollards In a way. Although I have to say it was my idea. (*Confidential*) Tell you the truth, Gillian. I've been a bit anxious about her lately, she seems a teensy bit — low (*with a nod towards the drinks cupboard*) if you get my meaning. Didn't like to leave her on her own.
Gillian She did fine on her own before.

Bollards She worries, you know, about her future with the show. Absurd, isn't it? I've told her it would all collapse without her.
Gillian Does — does she talk to you then?
Bollards I think it helps, don't you? Get it off your chest. When it's someone else in the business, who can understand. Can I get you something? While you're waiting? Oh, look, make yourself comfortable — go on, sit down, make yourself at home.
Gillian You frighten me, you really do. You freak me out. I'm scared if I let you get too close you'll suck me in and eat me whole.

Bollards stares at Gillian

Bollards Why, Gillian. What a very strange thing to say.
Gillian This isn't your house, do you hear me? It's Fay's house. Fay! Fay! Will you get down here? Fay, will you please come down!
Bollards Gillian. Dear. Whatever can be wrong?

Bollards puts her arms around Gillian and draws her to the sofa. Gillian shakes off the embrace and breaks away

Gillian Everything, everything, everything's all gone wrong.
Bollards It's all right. It's OK. Everything's going to be OK.

Allan appears at the bottom of the stairs, looking alarmed

It's fine, Allan, it's fine. Everything's fine. Gillian's just feeling a weeny bit upset but she's absolutely fine. Will you fetch her a glass of water?
Gillian I don't want any water.

Bollards nods

Allan exits into the kitchen

Bollards There now. There.
Gillian We were all OK. I don't understand what happened.
Bollards Nothing's happened. (*Producing a handkerchief and giving it to Gillian*) Here, have my hanky.

Gillian blows her nose and composes herself a little

Everything's perfectly fine.

Gillian offers to return the handkerchief

Act II, Scene 5   39

No, you keep it.
Gillian I needed to talk to Fay. I wasn't expecting you to be here.
Bollards I know, I know.

Allan enters with a glass of water which he puts on the table. He's anxious

Gillian I suppose I've upset Allan now.
Bollards We're all perfectly fine.

Bollards nods for Allan to leave

Allan backs out nervously into the hall

Gillian drinks

Gillian Oh dear, I don't usually … It's just so hard with the business the way it's been. It costs so much to run the office and keep everyone on and no contracts coming in. People just aren't recruiting at the moment. And there's a limit to how long you can hang on in there. Another month of this and we'll go bust. I'm not sleeping at night and in the day my brain's so addled I'm not really thinking straight. I shouldn't've let myself ring him. I know I must never ring him. His wife answered, of course she did, it's her house, she said who is that, who are you, who is that calling and I was so shocked I couldn't put the phone down. That was a week ago and he hasn't rung me. I won't hear from him again. I knew as soon as I heard her voice he'd never speak to me again.

Pause

Bollards Men. They always let you down. They either die, or dump you.

Gillian blows her nose again

Gillian Thanks. I shouldn't've said you freaked me out.
Bollards Ah well. We've all done things we've regretted later.

Gillian lets Bollards put her arm around her

Fay appears at the bottom of the stairs. She watches Bollards and Gillian

Bollards and Gillian look up and see Fay watching them. Gillian pulls away from Bollards

Gillian Fay. I was … I came to see you.

Bollards Aah. Here she is. Don't you look better. Did you have a lovely zizz? I hope so, dear.

Fay moves to the drinks cupboard and pours herself a glass of Scotch

Fay Either of you?
Bollards Oh I don't think the sun's quite over the yardarm yet, is it.
Gillian I will.

Fay comes to the sofas and sits

Bollards Gillian and I have been having a bit of a heart-to-heart. Rough patch.
Fay If you've come to ask for money again just say so. You can have a couple of thou but I don't want to hear how hard your life is, I'm not in the mood.
Gillian I wasn't actually going ——
Bollards Well, you know, Fay. It's like Mr Hudson used to say. Give a man a bowl of rice and you feed him for a day. Give him an ox and a plough and you feed him for life.
Fay I can't quite run to an ox and a plough.
Gillian I really wasn't going ——
Bollards Maybe it's not a handout she needs. So much as an investment in her company.
Gillian Bollards!
Fay You think so?
Gillian I would never dream — Fay, I swear to you. I'd never suggest such a thing.
Fay Well that's good. I wouldn't want to risk the good name of your business. With money from some trashy little show.
Gillian You know I ——
Fay Besides which. In my present uncertain situation, what I need is a rock solid portfolio. Unlikely to include the death-throe remnants of Eighties grab-it Britain.
Gillian (*standing*) I always thought you admired what I'd made of the business.
Fay (*standing*) I did. About as much as you admired my show.
Bollards Girls, girls. This is such a beautiful house. Let's not fall out in it.
Jude (*off; from the hall*) Hallo, Fay! Only me. It's letters time!

Jude enters

Well. Surprise. Hallo all. Are you having a party?

Black-out

Scene 6

The same. Not very much later

The Lights come up rapidly on the sofas. Fay, Gillian, Jude and Bollards are seated and each holds a hand of cards. Their body language is bad; Fay, Gillian and Jude are barely speaking to each other and Bollards is relentlessly upbeat. They have drinks glasses. Allan stands behind Jude so he can see her hand; he's trying to to teach them the game. He is uncomfortable

Allan OK. So you want the Triumph Vitesse.
Jude Why?
Allan Because Triumph is what you're collecting.
Jude Right.
Allan Go on, then.
Jude Has anyone got the Triumph Vitesse?
Allan No, *ask* someone.
Bollards It's like Happy Families, that's all. But with cars. Come on, you lot, you're all so depressed all the time — it's meant to be cheering us up.
Gillian Pity's sake.
Jude Fay. Have you got ——
Allan "Please may I have", you're supposed to say.
Jude — the Triumph Vitesse?
Fay (*showing a card to Allan*) Is that it?
Allan That's the GT6.
Fay No.
Allan Except you don't say no.
Fay Don't I?
Jude But she hasn't got it. Have you got it, Fay?
Fay No.
Allan You say, "Sorry, not at home."
Fay That's ridiculous.
Allan Ask her again.
Jude Have you got ——
Allan Please may I have.
Jude — the Triumph Vitesse?
Fay No.
Jude Have you got it, Bollards?
Bollards That's not right, you can't do that.
Jude Why not?
Bollards You can't just go round asking everyone, you'd be bound to get it then.

Jude I thought getting it was the point.
Gillian I've got it. (*She throws the card on the table*)
Allan Don't tell her!

Jude picks it up

Jude Thanks.
Gillian Who's got the Jaguar Mark 8 then?
Fay I have. (*She hands it over to Gillian*)
Bollards No, no! Give it back. It isn't even your turn.
Jude It's very complicated.
Fay It's my turn. I'm collecting Lotuses.
Jude How do you know you are?
Fay Might as well. Already got the Elise and Eclat. So Gillian. Have you got the Lotus Elan?
Gillian No. I've got a Riley you could have. (*She throws down a card*)
Allan You should've asked my mother, you see. She's the one's been collecting them.
Bollards Don't tell her!
Jude Can I have that Riley? (*She picks up Gillian's discarded card*)
Fay Right, Bollards. I want the Lotus Elan.
Allan It's too late. You can't ask her now!
Fay Hasn't she got it?
Allan Yes, but it's not your turn.
Bollards It's mine. Fay. Please may I have the Lotus Elise.

Fay hands a card over

Please may I have the Lotus Eclat.

Fay hands this one over more doubtfully

Please may I have the Jaguar Mark 8.

Fay selects this card and Bollards takes it from her

Fay Can she do that? Allan?
Bollards And please may I have the Triumph GT6.
Fay That's cheating, isn't it? (*She gives the card*)
Allan Well, actually ——
Bollards Thank you, Fay. Jude. Please may I have the Riley Monaco Saloon?
Jude That's not fair. You saw me pick it up.

Act II, Scene 6   43

Bollards You shouldn't've shown me then, should you?
Jude Well, I'm not going to give it to you. (*She throws all her cards down*)

Gillian peers at the cards

Gillian Is that a proper family?
Allan No, it's not.
Bollards I've seen those now.

Bollards throws her cards down

There's no point if you're not going to play properly.
Gillian Has Jude won then?
Bollards No, she hasn't.

Fay puts her cards down and smiles sweetly at Allan

Fay Well, thank you, Allan. I think we've finished now. We all seem much jollier, don't we?

Allan collects up the cards

Allan It is a good game actually. We used to play it with Dad.
Gillian I don't understand who won.
Fay Bollards has won. Fill that up, Jude, will you? (*She holds out her glass to Jude*)

Bollards intercepts the glass. She fills it with Allan's Lucozade and returns it

Well, see that. Isn't that kind? Bollards wants to save me from myself. Bollards wants to save all of us. Bollards is our guardian angel. Let's drink to Bollards!

Fay pours the Lucozade into the vase of flowers. It overflows on to the glass tabletop. Everyone watches the spreading pool. Pause

Gillian gets up to get herself a proper drink. Bollards stops her

Bollards There's something I want to say to you all. I hope you'll let me. We've known each other for ages, haven't we? We're really old friends. And old friends are just the best sort of all. They may take each other for granted sometimes. Hey, they may fall out. But in a pinch they'll always be there for each other. And that's what I wanted to talk to you about. Being there.

Gillian Ugh. She sounds like a *Frankly Fay* item.

Bollards You lot've been there for me these past few months, you really have. You can't know the difference you've made to my life. I'm a whole new woman, aren't I, Allan? You've picked me up and taken me in and, best of all, you've renewed our friendship. And when she invited me on her show, Fay opened up vistas in real life that I'd only seen in my dreams before. She's found talents I didn't know I had. And, and with great generosity, she's budged up and let me share an outlet for them. You've all been fantastic. I can never thank you enough.

Jude (*mumbling uncomfortably*) Oh dear.

Gillian (*mumbling uncomfortably*) Yes, well.

Fay (*mumbling uncomfortably*) Will someone get me out of here.

Bollards But I hate the tensions there are in the house. Oh, you maybe thought I was too thick to pick them up but I do, I feel them. And I excuse them too. Because I know what's behind them. I know why they're there. They're there because, as Jude I think it was wisely said, we all have our difficulties.

Fay Oh belt up, Bollards. Sit down, for pity's sake.

Bollards You can't shut me up that easily, Mr Hudson used to say ——

Gillian Well, get on with it then.

Bollards OK. Let's begin with Jude. Jude's difficulties are all because she's got nowhere to live ——

Jude I'm used to it now. I can manage. Please don't ——

Bollards A trailer is not a suitable residence for a woman with a first-class degree.

Jude I should never've ——

Bollards And all this time, while Allan and I are here looking after Fay, our little semi on the by-pass will just be standing there, empty. (*She produces her house keys and tosses them to Jude*) Sorted.

Jude Oh, no ——

Fay Now hang on a minute.

Bollards Don't you give it a second thought, Fay. It's our pleasure to look after you. Isn't it, Allan? And Jude'll be able to wallow in Assyrians to her heart's content.

Jude It's twenty years at least since I've done any work on that project. I mean, I've rather lost the thread.

Bollards Now's your chance then, isn't it, to pick it up.

Jude Oh.

Fay I can't have you and Allan ——

Bollards I'll be coming to you in a minute, Fay. But next it's Gillian.

Jude But I rather enjoyed Fay's letters.

Act II, Scene 6   45

Bollards Gillian's difficulties are that her business is going bust and she's been dumped by her married lover.
Gillian That was a confidence, Bollards.
Jude You didn't tell Bollards about William?
Fay Has the bastard really dumped you?
Gillian Oh God.
Bollards 'Fraid I can't conjure up a new admirer, Gilly. Unless of course Allan would like to pipe up at this point!
Allan Oh, no, I … No, no, I … No. Oh, no.
Gillian Oh, ground. Please open and swallow me up. Dearest ground.
Bollards But the business is quite a simple matter. Mr Hudson was a methodical man who took his family responsibilities seriously. There was sizeable Life Insurance in the event of his early death.
Fay Wait. You ran him over. And then you claimed the Life Insurance.
Bollards Oh dear me! Point taken! In fact one can run over any number of people, in the privacy of one's own drive, without incurring any penalty at all.
Fay Remarkable.
Bollards Providing of course — that it's an accident! The point being. That I have funds at my disposal. We've lived on the income, Allan and me. The capital is there untouched. And now, thanks to all of you, we have another income.
Gillian You have now. In a year, no-one will know who you are.
Jude We're fine how we are, Boll.
Bollards Apparently I have more faith in you than you have in me!
Fay Either way, you shouldn't lend it to Gillian.
Gillian Thanks, Fay.
Fay Never lend anything you'll need to have back.
Bollards I'm not offering to lend it to her.

Pause. Gillian is transfixed in fear and fascination

I'm proposing to buy into her business. In return for which, she makes me an equal partner.
Jude Good heavens.
Fay What do you know about recruitment?
Gillian Work with you, Bollards? Not in this universe.
Bollards I'd have a say in policy of course. But the day-to-day running would be yours.
Gillian Oh, big deal.
Bollards It is a big deal. You've already told me the alternative.

Pause

Allan It was an accident.
Bollards That's right, pet. It was.
Gillian I have to kill myself.
Fay Thank the Lord that's over. I need another drink.
Bollards Wait Fay, wait. You haven't heard my gift to you. I owe you more than any of the others. You've done so much for me. You've given me acclaim and purpose and confidence. You've made me everything I am today.
Fay Be my guest. I want nothing from you. I absolve you of all gratitude.
Bollards All my life, I've wanted to be your friend.
Fay You're my friend. Done. We're quits.
Bollards And now that I truly am, you've no idea how proud that makes me.
Fay Please, no more.
Bollards You're beautiful and you're talented. You have fame, you have fortune. You have a fabulous house and wonderful, wonderful friends. You already have everything.

Fay moves towards the Scotch bottle. Bollards catches her arm

The only think you lack. Is peace of mind. (*She lets go*)

Now Fay doesn't move

You're worried about the future. We've sat up far into the night and you've poured out your heart.
Gillian You've talked to *Bollards?*
Bollards You think you're too old. That you're losing your looks, you've been there too long, they're tired of you. You're afraid they're going to axe the show.
Jude Bollards, don't you think ——
Bollards Well, that's what I can give you, Fay. Peace of mind. Last week, Exec. Prod. took me to lunch. That's the Executive Producer of the show, girls. Imagine, we went to the Ivy. If you want, you can even have lobster at the Ivy. He's quite a gentleman, the Exec. Prod.. He paid me a lot of attention. And he talked to me like an equal. He said he thought our audience was a lot like me and he asked me my opinion. Me! So I told him. Right out front. I told him.
Fay What did you tell him?
Bollards I told him, well. If our audience is at all like me, Exec. Prod., it *prefers* a mature woman. The more "lived in", the better. It won't mind at all if her looks are on the wane. Normal women make them feel OK about themselves and they feel fond of them. What they respect is Life Experience. And you know what, Fay? He agreed with me. The Exec.

Prod. agreed with me. He leant across the table and he shook me by the hand. He raised his glass to me. He said, "Miss Pollard, thank you! Our show's on the brink of a new life, I know it is, just around the corner." And then he made a little joke, Fay. The Exec. Prod.! He said, Why don't I call you, *Candidly Caroline!* Oh Fay. For you, my dear, dear friend. Peace of mind!

There is absolute silence in the room

The cordless phone rings

Allan, Fay, Gillian and Jude walk slowly away as the Lights fade to a pool of light on Bollards

They exit

SCENE 7

The set of "Candidly Caroline"

The ringing stops

Bollards stands quietly for a moment, and then animates

Bollards Thank you so much, all of you, for the huge welcome you've given me, on this first edition of *Candidly Caroline*. I feel tremendously at home and I know we're going to have a lot of fun together. Next week I'll introduce you to an amazing woman whose rich husband left her to live in a trailer park for twenty years. But before I go there's someone else I have to thank, and I think you know who it is. My close friend and predecessor, the great Fay Finch, for her faith in me and her generosity — miss you, Fay, we all do!

There is applause, which Bollards quietens

As you all know, Fay's been my friend for an embarrassingly long time. Before she was even Finch in fact, but that's our little secret. I've written this for her. It's my special tribute.
    Old friends are the best,
    Between us are ties that bind.
    I hope you'll appear as my guest,
    For our lives shall be ever entwined.

During the following, her voice is gradually drowned out by a wave of applause

Old friends are the best,
They know us through and through.
Their love passes every test,
No matter what we do ...

The Lights fade

SCENE 8

Fay's living-room

The Lights come up on Bollards, completely alone. The applause fades to nothing

Allan enters from the stairs and comes uncertainly towards Bollards

Bollards Hallo pet.
Allan I'm afraid. I want my dad.
Bollards I'm a bit frightened too.
Allan Are we famous?
Bollards Yes, we are, pet. We're so famous, you wouldn't believe.
Allan I don't want to be famous.
Bollards Oh, you do, pet. You do. Just as soon as you get used to it, you're going to love it.
Allan Are you used to it?
Bollards Nearly, pet. Very nearly. We can have anything we want now, you know that?
Allan Anything?
Bollards You name it.
Allan Can we have a paint gun?
Bollards Why not.
Allan What about a brake pipe flare tool, a torque wrench and a hydraulic puller?
Bollards Absolutely.
Allan Can we have a trolley jack, a valve spring compressor, an engine hoist and a spline bit set? Can we have ramps and lamps and axle stands? Can we have a piston rewinder?
Bollards Oh, Allan. My pet. It's going to be a whole new life.

The Lights fade to one small pool on Bollards and Allan. Then snap to Black-out

FURNITURE AND PROPERTY LIST

ACT I
SCENE 1

On stage: Big modern sofas. *On them*: cushions
Chairs
Glass coffee table. *On it*: big red leatherbound book
Drinks cupboard containing glasses, bottle of Scotch, bottles of gin, bottle of Lucozade
Cordless telephone

SCENE 2

Off stage: Glass, and glass of tomato juice (**Jude**)
Cloths, container of salt (**Gillian** and **Jude**)

SCENE 3

Personal: **Allan**: half a dozen Dinky Toys

SCENE 4

No additional properties

SCENE 5

No additional properties

ACT II
SCENE 1

Set: Vacuum cleaner for **Bollards**

Personal: **Jude**: bag containing sheaf of typed letters and envelopes

SCENE 2

Set: Giant Dinky Car box, paints and brushes for **Allan**

Off stage: Tray of tea and elegant deli pastry (**Bollards**)

Scene 3

Personal: **Gillian**: bag

Scene 4

No additional properties

Scene 5

Set: Vase of flowers on table

Off stage: Magazines and crate of Dinky Cars (**Allan**)
Drying-up cloths and hot water bottles (**Bollards**)
Mixer (**Bollards**)
Pile of things (**Allan**)
Glass of water (**Allan**)

Personal: **Bollards**: handkerchief

Scene 6

Set: Hands of cards for **Fay**, **Gillian**, **Jude** and **Bollards**
Bottle of Lucozade for **Allan**

Personal: **Bollards**: house keys

Scene 7

No additional properties

Scene 8

No additional properties

LIGHTING PLOT

Practical fittings required: nil
One interior. The same throughout. Two main lighting states: sitting room and TV chat show studio

ACT I

To open: General interior lighting

Cue 1	**Fay**: "I'll never forgive you for this. Never." *Black-out*	(Page 9)
Cue 2	After a very short pause *Bring up general interior lighting*	(Page 9)
Cue 3	**Bollards**: "Unfortunately died." *Black-out*	(Page 16)
Cue 4	After a very short pause *Bring up general interior lighting*	(Page 16)
Cue 5	**Bollards**: " … to present your show about Grief." *Black-out*	(Page 20)
Cue 6	After a very short pause *Bring up general interior lighting*	(Page 20)
Cue 7	**Fay**: " … appear on my show?" Pause *Black-out*	(Page 23)
Cue 8	Big show music plays *Bring up bright TV studio lighting*	(Page 23)
Cue 9	**Bollards** walks out. Sound cuts out *Black-out*	(Page 23)

ACT II

To open: General interior lighting

Cue 10	**Bollards**: "… to come and talk to you." *Black-out*	(Page 29)

Cue 11	After a very short pause *Bring up general interior lighting*	(Page 29)
Cue 12	**Bollards**: " … each a teeny slice, do you?" *Black-out*	(Page 32)
Cue 13	After a very short pause *Bring up general interior lighting*	(Page 32)
Cue 14	**Gillian**: "Just do what we know you're good at …" *Black-out*	(Page 35)
Cue 15	Applause *Bring up bright TV studio lighting*	(Page 35)
Cue 16	**Gillian**: "Damn." *Fade lights to black-out*	(Page 36)
Cue 17	After a very short pause *Bring up general interior lighting*	(Page 36)
Cue 18	**Jude**: "Are you having a party?" *Black-out*	(Page 40)
Cue 19	After a very short pause Bring up general interior lighting	(Page 41)
Cue 20	Cordless phone rings *Fade lights to a pool on* **Bollards**	(Page 47)
Cue 21	**Bollards**: "No matter what we do …" *Fade lights to Black-out*	(Page 48)
Cue 22	When ready *Bring up general interior lighting*	(Page 48)
Cue 23	**Bollards**: "… a whole new life." *Fade lights to spot on* **Bollards** *and* **Allan**, *then snap to black-out*	(Page 48)

EFFECTS PLOT

ACT I

Cue 1	**Fay**: "Let's just drink." *Doorbell*	(Page 8)
Cue 2	**Gillian**: "Or their pizza." *Doorbell*	(Page 8)
Cue 3	**Bollards** (*off*): "Anybody ho-ome?" *Door knocker*	(Page 8)
Cue 4	Black-out at end of SCENE 4 *Big show music*	(Page 23)
Cue 5	The lights come up on **Fay** *Segue music into loud applause, which dies away*	(Page 23)
Cue 6	**Fay**: " … the *amazing*, Caroline Pollard!" *Tremendous applause; show music*	(Page 23)
Cue 7	**Bollards** walks out into the light *Cut sound*	(Page 23)

ACT II

Cue 8	**Bollards** exits with the vacuum cleaner *Cordless phone rings*	(Page 25)
Cue 9	**Bollards** embraces **Jude** *Cordless phone rings*	(Page 28)
Cue 10	Black-out at end of SCENE 3 *Applause*	(Page 35)
Cue 11	The lights come up on the sofas *Fade applause*	(Page 35)
Cue 12	**Bollards**: "Has sealed our Fate." *Pause, then massive, prolonged applause*	(Page 36)

Cue 13	**Gillian**: "Damn." *Fade applause*	(Page 36)
Cue 14	**Bollards**: "Peace of mind!" Silence *Cordless phone rings*	(Page 47)
Cue 15	When ready *Cut phone ring*	(Page 47)
Cue 16	**Bollards**: " … miss you, Fay, we all do!" *Applause*	(Page 47)
Cue 17	**Bollards** gestures to quieten the applause *Applause fades*	(Page 47)
Cue 18	**Bollards**: " … shall be ever entwined." *Bring up applause over following dialogue, drowning it out*	(Page 47)
Cue 19	The lights come up on **Bollards** *Fade applause to nothing*	(Page 48)

A licence issued by Samuel French Ltd to perform this play does not include permission to use Incidental music. Where the place of performance is already licensed by the PERFORMING RIGHT SOCIETY a return of the music used must be made to them. If the place of performance is not so licensed then application should be made to the Performing Right Society, 29 Berners Street, London W1.

A separate and additional licence from PHONOGRAPHIC PERFORMANCES LTD, 1 Upper James Street, London W1R 3HG is needed whenever commercial recordings are used.

www.ingramcontent.com/pod-product-compliance
Ingram Content Group UK Ltd.
Pitfield, Milton Keynes, MK11 3LW, UK
UKHW021848210426
5322IPUK00022B/530